T0129428

Alone but Not Lonely

*Reclaim Your Identity and
Be Unapologetically You*

ROBIN JOY MEYERS

BALBOA.
PRESS

A DIVISION OF HAY HOUSE

This book is a work of non-fiction. Unless otherwise noted, the author and the publisher make no explicit guarantees as to the accuracy of the information contained in this book and in some cases, names of people and places have been altered to protect their privacy.

Balboa Press books may be ordered through booksellers or by contacting:

Balboa Press
A Division of Hay House
1663 Liberty Drive
Bloomington, IN 47403
www.balboapress.com
1 (877) 407-4847

Because of the dynamic nature of the Internet, any web addresses or links contained in this book may have changed since publication and may no longer be valid. The views expressed in this work are solely those of the author and do not necessarily reflect the views of the publisher, and the publisher hereby disclaims any responsibility for them.

The author of this book does not dispense medical advice or prescribe the use of any technique as a form of treatment for physical, emotional, or medical problems without the advice of a physician, either directly or indirectly. The intent of the author is only to offer information of a general nature to help you in your quest for emotional and spiritual well-being. In the event you use any of the information in this book for yourself, which is your constitutional right, the author and the publisher assume no responsibility for your actions.

Any people depicted in stock imagery provided by Thinkstock are models, and such images are being used for illustrative purposes only.
Certain stock imagery © Thinkstock.

Print information available on the last page.

ISBN: 978-1-5043-9648-6 (sc)
ISBN: 978-1-5043-9650-9 (hc)
ISBN: 978-1-5043-9649-3 (e)

Library of Congress Control Number: 2018901047

Balboa Press rev. date: 01/25/2018

CONTENTS

This book is dedicated to the two strongest women who have been my role models: my daughter, Kyra Jeanne, whose friendship, passion, beauty, strength, and heart are beyond words, and my mother, Jeanne, who passed away too young but gave me a foundation and a friendship for twenty-one years.

INTRODUCTION

Alone but Not Lonely is a story of reclaiming your identity, living unapologetically you and a guide to help you do so. When you are alone, it is a powerful time to reflect, plan, and quiet the outside noises so you can let your creativity soar.

Often, women compromise themselves to please or to do things for others. Whether this is for our families, friends, or bosses, it doesn't matter. It takes a lot of courage to stand steadfast and not to compromise ourselves to please others. Sometimes this causes an inner conflict that requires us to change past patterns and behaviors and to acknowledge our feelings. Whether you consider yourself to be an introvert, extrovert, or an ambivert (a combination of both types), at some point, you have struggled with the issues of self-worth, confidence, and a loss of self.

In a tribe, women tend to put their own needs after others. That's no surprise, especially since they are nurturers and caretakers. No matter how society defines women's roles, there is a natural instinct that bonds all women together.

This book is for women who feel like they need to have it all yesterday, who don't have it all, or who feel like they have lost their identity. Guess what? It is time to reclaim your identity and put you first. It is time to change your mind-set and to schedule happiness and self-preservation on your calendar.

How do you define lonely? Is it a sad time when no one is around or a room full of people you are too introverted or uncomfortable to be with? According to Wikipedia, the definition of loneliness is as follows: "*Loneliness* is a complex and usually unpleasant emotional response to isolation. *Loneliness* typically includes anxious feelings about a lack of connection or communication with other beings, both in the present and extending into the future. Some have defined loneliness as a disease." (https://en.wikipedia.org/wiki/Loneliness)

Although loneliness is a common human emotion, it is also a complex and unique experience for each individual. It has no single common cause, so the prevention and treatment for this damaging state of mind differs considerably. For example, a child, who tries to make friends at school, needs different strategies to resolve his or her problems than an elderly person, who has lost his or her spouse in the recent past, does.

To understand loneliness, it is important to have a closer look at exactly what we mean by the term *loneliness*. In this connotation, loneliness means isolation.

This book will help you understand that there are two states of loneliness. The first state is isolation. This is usually not a choice and carries a more negative connotation. This isolation can often be very lonely, negative, and unpleasant. The second state is solitude. This kind of loneliness is not lonely. It can be a choice and can be life giving, if you are a person who enjoys the comfort of being on your own time and in your own thoughts. In my life, *lonely* or *loneliness* has taken on many definitions and images, both in the state of isolation and the state of solitude.

However, until I made a conscious decision to give myself permission to let go and reclaim my identity, I did not realize that I was the one who had the power to make the difference for myself. This book is not to negate any circumstances that may have happened in the past. However, the purpose of *Alone but Not Lonely* is to show you that you can choose *not* to be a victim of your circumstances. Some call it breaking the cycle. I am in no way trying to make light of what you have gone through, but I am putting the power back into your hands. I want to empower you to be your own hero and realize that you are the only one that has the power to do so.

Being alone isn't always lonely and doesn't need to be. Being alone can be powerful, satisfying, and liberating. This book is my story and journey of just that. It is a story of my struggles to get to a place of strength, to move past those feelings of isolation, how and why I do what I do now, and when and how I chose to be the most authentic me.

I want you to know how to feel aligned and be the most powerful you. *Alone but Not Lonely* is about finding that alignment and changing your mindset so you can create the life you want to live.

How do you go about finding your self-worth, happiness, and confidence while discovering your passions? We will take a journey through stories and strategies so you can learn the answer to these things and become comfortable with yourself.

There are many avenues in this book, as you will see, but one of those avenues and the impetus to wanting to share my story and help others, was my own loneliness. I needed to take this journey to understand, recognize, and give myself permission to be who I wanted to be, without asking anyone else for his or her permission to do so.

I promise to be truly honest and authentic with you, the reader. I will be as real as I can be. I have experienced depression, anxiety, suicidal thoughts, horrible jobs, bad relationships, many losses, and so forth. Through them, I have learned that I needed an advocate. First and foremost, that advocate was me. We must be our own heroes and our own best friends.

The book is also a compilation of other people's stories and definitions when asked, "What does alone but not lonely mean to you?" I asked friends as well as random individuals that question. Their answers varied tremendously but overall, my goal was that they tell their stories of their journeys and struggles—what turned loneliness into their precious quality alone time.

To get to the end result, you have to be very comfortable with the person you are and clear about what you want. It doesn't mean you have to have it all buttoned up, but it does mean you have the right mind-set for yourself. It's recognizing and getting rid of the self-sabotage as well as finding your passion and identity. It's giving yourself permission to be unapologetically you!

This book is divided into three main parts. The first part is the foundation for and the theory of what *Alone but Not Lonely* means. The second part is filled with practical tools and strategies to help you change the way you think and make changes in your life. The final part is filled with stories I have gathered from those who wanted to share their trials and tribulations of being alone, in both a negative and positive manner.

As you go through the book, my hope is to help you understand when loneliness is coming from a perspective of isolation versus empowerment. So if you're ready, let's start on this journey together.

PART 1

Theory

Understanding the Concept of Loneliness

It is estimated that over 40 percent of us will feel the aching pangs of loneliness at some point in our lives. Yet despite how common loneliness is, few people are fully aware of the dramatic ways it impacts us. Here are ten surprising facts about loneliness that will change how you view this all-too-common but devastating psychological condition:

1. Loneliness does not depend on how many friends or relationships we have.

Loneliness depends entirely on the *subjective* quality of our relationships and whether we feel emotionally and/or socially disconnected from those around us. That is why ...

2. More than 60 percent of lonely people are married.

When married couples no longer share their deepest feelings, thoughts, and experiences with their spouses, it can leave them feeling disconnected and alone. A person who is in this type of relationship truly believes his or her spouse cannot offer the deep connection this individual would like. While this person's fears might be correct, they might also stem from the fact that the individual has not allowed for time to find his or her true passions.

3. Loneliness distorts our perceptions of our relationships.

Studies have found that asking people to recall times they felt lonely was sufficient to make them devalue their relationships. These perceptual distortions often cause lonely people to withdraw even further from the very people who could alleviate their loneliness.

4. Loneliness is contagious in social networks.

Loneliness has a clear stigma: When we are lonely, we tend to be able to spot and to identify the lonely people around us. One study found that over a six-month period, lonely people were pushed to the periphery of social networks and surprisingly, so were their friends. Being pushed out this way into the cold has a surprising effect on our feelings of self-worth and self-esteem.

5. Loneliness actually makes us feel colder.

Studies found that recalling a time in which they felt lonely made participants feel a drop in the room temperature. It even made their actual skin temperature colder. The idea of feeling pushed into the cold resonates from our evolutionary past, in which being ostracized from our tribes meant being kept away from the warmth of the hearth and the social group around it.

6. Loneliness makes our bodies feel like they are under attack.

Loneliness causes an immediate and severe bodily reaction. It increases blood pressure and cholesterol and activates our physical and psychological stress responses. Loneliness can increase feelings of fatigue, depression, and sadness.

7. Chronic loneliness significantly increases our risk of cardiovascular disease.

Over time, people who are chronically lonely have a much higher incidence of cardiovascular disease because their bodies are under constant and unrelenting stress.

8. Loneliness suppresses our immune systems.

Loneliness causes our immune systems to function less efficiently. Over time, this puts us at an increased risk for developing all kinds of illnesses and diseases.

9. College freshmen who felt lonely had poorer reactions to flu shots.

Even a few weeks of loneliness impacted the immune systems of incoming college freshman, so much so that they had poorer reactions to seasonal flu shots than those who were not lonely. Loneliness impacts our bodies just like stress can.

10. Loneliness is as dangerous as cigarette smoking.

Scientists have concluded that given all the drastic ways in which loneliness impacts our bodies, it represents as great a risk for our long-term health and longevity as smoking cigarettes. Indeed, studies have concluded that chronic loneliness increases our risk of an early death by 14 percent.[2]

Clearly, loneliness represents an important psychological injury that you should not ignore. Therefore, make sure you recognize any negative triggers when you are lonely. You also need to educate others who are lonely about the dangers of remaining that way. Again, this state of loneliness refers to isolation.

Understanding the *Concept of Loneliness* in terms of solitude can be very empowering. Being able to be still with yourself allows you a certain clarity and transparency to learn more about you. Solitude is defined as the state of being alone or on your own. Solitude can also refer to a place where you're completely alone. The middle of the woods, the top of a big mountain, the middle of a vast desert, even your room — these are places where you might go for solitude. Solitude suggests peacefulness stemming from a state of inner richness. It is a means of enjoying the quiet and whatever it brings that is satisfying and from which we draw sustenance. It is something we can cultivate which is refreshing as well as an opportunity to renew ourselves. In other words, it replenishes us. (https://www.psychologytoday.com/articles/200307/what-is-solitude)

CHAPTER 1

My Story

Most people tiptoe through life hoping
we safely make it to death.

—Earl Nightingale

Ponder that statement for a moment. What does it mean to you? Are you playing the game of life and going through the motions but are not really energized by it? If this is what you are doing, this book is definitely for you.

We hear, so often, that life is too short! Well, that's sort of true. Life is too short. You may not realize and appreciate that until you are middle-aged like I am at fifty-three—although quite honestly, I do not think

◇

fifty-three is middle-aged. Maybe it's because I am that age now, but for me the Fifties feel like the new Forties. It's not that I feel old. In fact, I have never felt better about myself. It took approaching the age of fifty for me to think, *Holy shit! If I am healthy, then I am halfway there.* I realized I had a chance to look at my own personal crossroads.

So I turned my head to the left and looked at the first half of my life. Did I like what I saw? Was I happy with the first half? I was married at twenty-six, and it seemed idyllic at that time. My husband had been living outside of Washington DC. Because I was young and in love and that was where my husband wanted to live, that was where I went—no questions asked. Today, it would be a whole different story. Today, I would expect that we would choose together where we were going to live, but back then, I was still that little girl who was always aiming to please.

We spent too much time focusing on and worrying about money. I think money is a typical trap that married couples fall into. For a couple, finances are a reality. Many marriages dwell on this. Now I know that you can only control what you can control. We had our worries, yet we never truly sat down and faced finances head on. Couples have so many tools they can use—even one as simple as a budget. However, we complained and made no effort to rectify the situation.

Through the fun times and hard times of being young and in love, raising three children, fast forward

◇

to my children's young adult phase when my youngest, my daughter, was a freshman in high school and my middle son was a junior. My oldest was already in college, so tuition bills had started. I certainly hadn't planned the timing of my children's births very well. Having to pay two tuitions simultaneously for a long time would be interesting. However, I did take a good look at my life. My first and most rewarding career was motherhood. Absolutely no doubt about it. I loved being a mother and was fortunate enough to be able to be home so I could participate in all my children's activities.

***

Have you ever thought about what you would be worth if you added up your hours doing daily chores and obligations. Whether you are a stay-at-home mother, a career mother, or a caretaker of an older parent, just think about how much money you would make if you were paid for it. One of my workshops is called Know Your Worth. It would be fun, from the perspective of a mother, to add up a woman's worth based on her talents as the family's CEO, chef, chauffeur, personal shopper, and so much more. By looking up salaries on various job portals, I found that the average income a woman would make is $100 thousand dollars a year. For example, on www.salary.com a personal chef's salary can range between seventy and ninety thousand

◇

dollars. Chauffeur salaries range between forty to seventy dollars per hour. Imagine that!

***

Because my husband and I needed to pay two simultaneous college tuitions, I needed to shift gears to the work-outside-the-home mentality. This was challenging but also a common experience for many women. First of all, I needed to find my work and life balance. That was not going to happen overnight after being home for sixteen years. The other challenge was the type of job I would be qualified for. I had a master of science in molecular genetics, but what was that going to translate to? I also wanted to have a somewhat flexible job so that I could still be near my kids, especially after school.

Well, a close friend made my résumé look good, and that's when my journey started. As often as I speak about how my college path would not be something I would ever choose now, I must say that it has shaped the person that I have become today.

So that's what happened when I looked to the left. When I looked to the right at the next fifty years, I thought, *Please, God, it better be much more fun in terms of exciting and engaging*. It's not that life wasn't fun, but what did I want to do? What hadn't I accomplished? Was I enjoying life? Who, in the hell, was Robin Joy Meyers? She was just me—not his wife or

◇

their mom or even that dog's owner—just me! What did I want the next fifty years to look like?

I did know this: I wanted life to be fun, exciting, engaging, less worrisome, and light. I wanted to figuratively and literally drop the excess baggage in terms of my job and responsibilities and maintenance of a big home. I didn't need the big house filled with too many televisions and other material items. I wanted to make every day count. I wanted life to be meaningful. I wanted to feel that everyday I made someone else's life a little bit more positive.

We have all created bucket lists, as I did. Near the top of my list were travel, cooking, and theater. I wanted to see the world, learn about new cultures, and appreciate the joy of life as well as give that joy to others.

Let me break down my story because in order to really share my journey, you need to travel in my shoes for a moment. My story seemed to be saying that to find inner peace I needed to look at my past. I did this by dividing my story into the sections that follow and sharing them. My hope is that by sharing my experiences, you will find my stories relatable and engaging so that they offer insight into your own journey; past, present and future.The sections that present my story start with my childhood, go through my young adult and teenage years, and finish at the age of fifty-two. It wasn't until I was fifty-two that I got it and really owned it. Finally, I recognized that I could determine the path I chose my life to take. My journey was my own story to craft, write and tell. In order for me to give you anything of value, I have had to put peace and closure to each of the four life stages that I present and encourage you to do the same.

To truly find inner peace, you need to make amends with your past by taking time for self-reflection. This will happen as you are willing and happy to embrace being alone but not lonely. I reiterate that this is the part where you really need to let go! Have no regrets and do not say, "I wish that I had done that differently."

As I have allowed that process to occur, I have learned a lot about myself, and that is a process unto itself. What has happened is in the past, and if anything, learn from it. If you do not want it to reoccur, break the cycle by being aware of it. Know the triggers and warning signs and understand the mind-set that got you there. It is a huge win for you when you can accomplish this. The awareness and sense of being alive will all begin to factor into the process as you become comfortable with you and recognize your happiness.

So what have I done so far? Well, that's easy to answer! Not nearly as much as I wanted to. I haven't traveled to many places in my adult, married life. I was fortunate enough to travel to Hawaii for our honeymoon, and we were able to take the family to Jamaica and the beach. Although these are wonderful opportunities, not all wonderful things lead to fulfillment. However, because we had three children and no priority to travel, even though it was one of my passions, needs, and

◇

desires, it never happened. I always wanted and still would love to live abroad for even one month.

There was always an excuse. Whether it was money, my husband's job, or school, we did not make our family's vacations a priority. In some regards, my kids were gypped. If I was able to go back and give my children advice for their future families, I would tell them to forget the material gifts and to prioritize going on unique vacations during their holidays and the summertime each year if possible. I am sure my kids would have remembered going on them much more than the thousands of Pokémon cards, dolls, or gaming systems that we purchased.

So in my next fifty plus years, I want and plan to travel, especially to fulfill my desire to cook my way through Europe—specifically in Italy, Greece, and Spain. I want to travel with my daughter around the world and across the country, just embracing time. So, how, in the hell, am I going to make that happen?

Let me break down my story, because in order to really share my journey, you need to travel through my childhood, while living at home, to my college years, through my young adult and graduate school life, up until marriage through the present. It wasn't until I was fifty-three that I got it and really owned it. So in order for me to give you anything of value, I have had to put peace and closure on each of my four life stages and encourage you to do the same.

My challenge to you is to reflect on and answer the

◇

following quote: *"Can you remember who you were, before the world told you who you should be?"* (Danielle LaPorte)

***

As I reflect on my lessons learned, I encourage you to do the same. In summary, here are three important elements to be aware of as you begin to claim your identity and define what *Alone but Not Lonely*, in all its power, means to you. What is your story?

Prioritize You

An important element in finding you and your alignment is to prioritize you and your needs. Women, you have to be the ones to do this for yourselves. No one will offer this to you, so you must know your sense of self.

No Regrets

Begin to shift the negative connotation associated with the word "regret." Instead of looking at regrets as failure, shift your thought process to be kinder and more compassionate to yourself, recognizing that you have grown from that past situation. Remember that no matter how big or small that moment may have been, it contributed to the person that you have become today.

◇

Developing the ability to look back and be completely honest with yourself is a huge step forward.

Define Who You Are

As women, life can be busy and full of transitions. We wear many hats, which represent the different roles we play on a daily basis, such as partner, career person, parent, widow, or divorcee. However, remember to always put yourself first. Whatever role in life you are playing at this very moment, the most important role is *you*, which requires self-preservation. Remember earlier I mentioned my desire to feel alive and not just be alive. Embrace yourself for being you and approach your journey as an exercise in self-preservation.

What happens when you look back at your life? You have to give yourself permission to move forward, acknowledging past, present, and future desires.

***

Life Stage #1

The Beginning

(Birth to Age Eighteen)

This first stage covers a large span of years. These years are grouped under the concept of living at home.

Looking at this stage can help us see the foundations for some of the decisions we made later in life.

Here is my story and what I learned at this stage. Take a moment to reflect on your own story and what you learned at this stage of your life. I encourage you to ask yourself what advice you would give to the six-year-old you.

Before I start, I need to say one more thing. I hope that you have many more memories of your childhood than I do. I know I had a happy childhood, but I do not have a vivid box of memories. I hope I have done a better job with my own three children in giving them a childhood that they will remember.

My parents were not bad at all. They were fantastic and loving. In fact, my mother and I were incredibly close. With that being said, it seems as if there was always a protective shield around me. Maybe they thought I would crumble under any hardships, which is rather ironic. All families have hardships at some point.

Let's be realistic. Overall, I had a relatively normal childhood, but I was very introverted. I was a goody-two-shoes as my brothers would say. I was always ready to call them out for whatever wrong they were committing.

My young childhood was typical of the area that I grew up in. I was very fortunate and privileged to have such amenities as Girl Scouts, horses, theater, and Hebrew school three times a week. My parents gave me a bat mitzvah.

◇

I went to a private school from eighth grade through high school. My private school was interesting. It was incredibly small, and although we were financially comfortable, many children who were much wealthier than I was attended the school. If you compare it to the movie *Mean Girls*, it was an older version of that. I tried to be a cheerleader and to play sports. I even participated in the theater productions but spent those years scared of my own shadow.

In my senior year, I tried to be social. I was fortunate enough to travel abroad to France with my French class. After four to five years of French, I could order French fries effectively.

I remember senior prom and how all I wanted to do was skip it. I didn't have a date at first, and then I had a date I didn't want. Yet somehow, I went and had an awful time. In fact, I remember calling my mom to see how her night was going because I was so bored with mine. That is when they had pay phones by the bathrooms.

In tenth grade, I was asked to the senior prom by a fun, outgoing, and funny senior. He was absolutely adorable, but that relationship didn't last very long. I blew that quickly. I was afraid to ask my parents if I could stay out late. In fact, the *after party*, which my kids all went to, was a nightmare for the poor guy and me as well. Let's just say I was immature, and it showed. I share this with you because lets face it. Most of us have horror stories about high school relationships,

◇

friendships, or prom. However, in my life this behavior was a pattern and when I realized this pattern only then was I able to acknowledge and move forward.

This is how I lived through my high school years. I certainly didn't come close to falling in with the cool group or any group, for that matter, and spent many weekend nights hanging out at home—not that anything was wrong with that.

I remember my mother, who really was my best friend, would remind me that it was better to have one truly good friend than a roomful of acquaintances. I was always a *leader* and never a follower. In fact, in my adult life, I have a handful of truly good friends. I don't need a huge group to hang with even now as an adult.

So when I graduated from high school, I went from the New York City area to major culture shock in a place called Hiram, Ohio. Can you imagine it? Take a girl who is already scared to death of life and let her go off to the middle of nowhere to hide some more. Can you guess where this next stage will go?

***

I want to side bar this section, because as I told you, this was a fast flashback into my childhood. There's not a whole lot more to tell except this: I had the opportunity to model and be exposed to the fashion and the theater world. My father was in the garment industry and had a showroom in midtown Manhattan. I was in the city at least three times a week as a teenager, and during the

◇

summer months, I worked in my father's showroom. That too was a very lonely time for me.

I was in the center of New York's fashion scene. However, my parents didn't want me exposed to that world. Clothing buyers would come into the showroom and ask for the line to be presented. Instead of allowing me to model the clothes, my parents would bring other people into the office or ask the receptionist to do this. I didn't have the guts to beg my father, but I am not sure that would have made a difference or not. I think, in many ways, he thought that he was protecting me. However, looking back, I often wonder if he was actually hiding me.

I had many opportunities but unlike my children, thank goodness, didn't reach for a dream or passion. If I had had the tools then that I have now as an adult, I think I would have suffered less depression and loneliness. I challenge you to look back at your childhood and ask yourself what would you say to your younger self?

***

◇

Life Stage #2

The Middle

(Age Eighteen through Twenty-One)

In this second stage, we are on the cusp of adulthood. Legally, we are of age; however, statistics show that a young adult's brain is not mature until the ages of twenty-three to twenty-six. Some of us have gone to college. Others entered the work world. Looking at this stage can help us see the foundations for some of the decisions we made later.

Below is my story and what I had learned at this stage. Take a moment to create your own reflections from your story and what you learned at this stage of life.

Let me start by describing my first experience of driving into Hiram College in Hiram, Ohio, in September 1982. Hiram is about one hour west of Youngstown, Ohio, and one hour east of Cleveland, Ohio. After about seven hours of driving, I came up this huge hill. As I approached the top, there was a traffic light, which was green. I happened to be driving with my mom. The foliage was gorgeous. There were beautiful trees and hills with yellow and red colors. It was absolutely breathtaking, especially since most of the drive had been flat, straight roads.

We blew through the traffic light and traveled for another fifteen minutes. We began to see signs for another town, which had not been on our radar. This is going to date me, but this was when you had paper maps from AAA and no GPS system. We ended up stopping at a gas station where they told us to go back to the one traffic light we had just driven through. At the light, we were to turn right and there we would find Hiram: the whole town and college. I basically freaked out and thought, *WTF! Maybe I should just drive back to New York.* Anyway, that was just the beginning of my culture shock like no other I had experienced before.

It was also the beginning of a weird time of loneliness, personal conflict, and wondering who I was. Yes, I was eighteen—but a very immature eighteen. College is all about going out and exploring new things. It's about meeting new people and stepping out of your comfort zone. Well, I think you can imagine how this was for me. I would rather go eat by myself or stay in my dorm room.

Hiram was very small, but we did have one social hall/bar on campus. It was today's version of a student center but on a smaller scale. Keep in mind that my high school was tiny. I graduated with fifty-one students, so a college of 1,350 people was more than I was used to. I did not know even one person who went there. Meeting new people was not my forte. I had met numerous people from the New Jersey area who had appeared to be interesting. Yet, I didn't really understand why people would willingly subject themselves to this culture shock.

◇

I did have a roommate, but that only lasted three days. She ended up locking me out on the first night because she hooked up with some guy. I thought not having a roommate was great. I ended up with a single room, which I thought was fantastic. I didn't have to answer or speak to anyone.

Instead of meeting people, I thought I should be studying. Just like in high school, I would come back from class or dinner and study. When I was done, I went to bed. It was not a good way to go make friends but a good way to isolate myself. I was also homesick.

I was trying to please my parents, who lived eight hours away, by studying hard, because I was planning on getting a degree in the sciences. Let me just tell you now that I was a good student but not fantastic or naturally smart. I had to work for my grades, and I was a horrible standardized test taker.

To make a long, boring story short, I didn't begin to enjoy college until the end of my junior year. I started to go out more and even party a little bit. All was good and nothing bad happened to me. In fact I actually enjoyed myself and still continued to get the same grades as before. I actually started to grow up and mature. Shocking, right? It was about time. The unfortunate thing was that, in some ways, it was a little too late. I chose to be alone and lonely to a fault. I isolated myself. I thought that I had to focus on college work and classes. That's what my parents expected of me.

⟺

However, I realize now that I created that falsehood. I put those parameters on me—not my parents or anyone else. I want you all to remember that. I used my books as an excuse and a way to hide from the world. That was so far from what the college experience was supposed to be. Accepting and acknowledging that fact has helped me move forward in accepting my quirkiness, weirdness, or whatever you want to label it as. I did not find my voice. I am not sure I can put the blame on my childhood, birth order, family, or parents.

***

Undoubtedly, please remember this: *You have a voice, so use it!* It has been my experience, while teaching and coaching young adults, that they are typically too timid to ask questions and to use their voices. This is because society has given them the perception that they're old enough to advocate for themselves but that there is a fine line between doing that and being rude.

No matter what the situation may be, you have the right to use your voice. Sometimes we do need to be more respectful; however, always ask. The worst thing that can happen is someone says no to your question. Oh well!

One of my greatest losses in college was that I was so guarded (like armor) I did not grow up and mature. I avoided social situations. I lost friendships and even the opportunity for love. Some of those friendships have rekindled over the past several years, which I am

◇

so grateful for. It has been fun for me to hear people's stories and about their lives and to share my stories as well.

***

On a side note, I look at my children, who have graduated and are now working in their various worlds. As a parent, I am so proud of them and their confidence. One son graduated from college and spent a month traveling throughout Europe with his friends. My other son is truly an entrepreneur. My youngest child is the strongest woman I know. She is pursuing her dream and passion for the arts, and no one—and many have tried—will stand in her way. I'm not sure if I had any influence but am so proud of each of them. Reflecting back on when I was their age, was I following my dream of becoming a Geneticist or was I following someone else's expectations? I know that I did not have the self-confidence and sense of self-worth in my earlier years.

So, what are my expectations for myself in this next part of my life? Possibly follow the example my children have set and do what they are doing during this next part of my life. I wish that I had lived abroad in my twenties. How fun would that have been? I still plan to live abroad for even a month within the next ten years. Life does not have to be scripted for you. You get to write that script. You also have the ability to edit that script. Embrace change!

***

◇

Let's step back into college. I was still studying and trying to prove I was a good science student, so the next step was to apply to medical school. Remember what I said before? I was a horrible standardized test taker and not as smart as I had thought I was. I was a good student but not great. Honestly! I tried to work hard but didn't enjoy college until the end of my junior year.

How do you think I did on the Medical College Admission Test, otherwise know as the MCAT? Of course, I didn't get into medical school. I failed my MCAT, so I decided to stay in science and to attend graduate school in hopes that I could reapply in a year or two after receiving my master's degree. Somebody should have sat me down and stopped me.

Here's another twist. The night before I left to go to graduate school in Cleveland, Ohio, I received my acceptance letter to New York Medical College's genetic counseling program. Being a stubborn twenty-year-old, I had a choice. I could move ten hours away so I could be on my own in Cleveland, Ohio, or change it up and live forty-five minutes away from my parents. I chose to keep my plans and move back to Ohio. The apartment was ready, and I thought I was so confident. Yet all I did was fuel my loneliness.

I became the rebellious graduate student and moved into my first apartment in Cleveland, Ohio. Now I was defying my parents, especially my mom. My mother virtually begged me to stay in New York and told me that the genetic counseling program would be the best route

◇

for me to take. It probably was, however, again, I can't go back. If I had become a genetic counselor, I probably would never have done what I am doing now. I will never know, so there is no reason to dwell on that notion.

My mother and I were very close but still in a mother-child relationship. We never transitioned into a more adult relationship. Again, I am not sure if that is what she wanted and created or if I did. Maybe in some ways we both created our relationship to be that way. That will make better sense later on, so hold onto that thought. I should mention that my dad and I had a good relationship, but I was so close to my mom I didn't rely on my Dad. He was always working, so I guess it was a typical relationship.

Reflecting back on this time, I wish I had been a little more adventurous and had traveled the world more. I was still playing by the rules. An interesting question would be, who wrote those rules? Was I playing by someone else's rules or by my own self-inflicted ones? As a side note, this is the area in which I know my children are much more savvy in than I ever was.

Even when I was a graduate student, I took my work and schedule very seriously. I had to be the first person in the lab. I got a little bit better at speaking to people and socializing but not great.

However, I did make a conscious decision one day. I told myself that I could either be alone and lonely or I could put myself out there and do things. Alone, at this point, meant literally being in my apartment by myself.

I hadn't figured out what my needs and desires were. I wish I had taken trips, cooked my way through Europe, and so forth, but I hadn't been ready or savvy enough to redefine myself yet.

As I started to find my rhythm in graduate school, I dealt with my self-sabotage. You all know that little voice inside your head spreading negative feelings of doubt, guilt, and shame. Well my little voice was screaming at me. The result was that the other side of lonely became a little darker and much more personal. I truly believe that's when I started to fight depression, and my loneliness was coming from a place of isolation. Although I sought help from a counselor for approximately four months, I was always having a cheery, protected conversation. It was really self-deprecating and pointless, because even though this "professional" was paid to listen and advise, I would not let my guard down. It triggered those childhood memories of keeping information private.

In May 1988, my mother went to the doctor because she hadn't been feeling well. I called on my lab's phone to see how her appointment had gone. My dad said that the appointment had not gone well. When I pushed for more information, he told me to come home that weekend. So I booked my usual flight from Cleveland to Newark. When I arrived, I found out that my mother had been diagnosed with multiple myeloma, which, at the time, was a rare form of cancer.

This shook my world. My emotions were all over

◇

the place. Selfishly, I started to create my life, yet my mother was ill. I felt like I was being pulled in so many directions, however either direction led me to a feeling of isolation. Supposedly, everything was going to be okay. I still went back and forth from graduate school in Ohio to my parents' house in New York a few times. My responsibilities as a Master's student required me to focus on my research project and thesis, so in some regards I was obviously obligated to work even through the summer months. However, it also allowed me to isolate myself even further by just burying myself in my work.

One Thursday in September, I received a call from my father. He told me that I should come home. My mom was in the hospital, and things were not looking great. The next thing I knew, I was back on a United flight at 6:00 a.m., because it had been too late in the night to find a flight on Thursday.

My mother passed away very early Saturday morning at the age of fifty-three. My immediate family started to disintegrate. Nobody really wanted to talk about or tell anyone of her passing. I was back to being lost again. Let me just point out that my family members were not the best communicators. This had been true as far back as I could remember. Their way of dealing with this tremendous loss was not to talk about it.

Life became rather tricky for me in a number of ways. First, I was twenty-one and had lost my best friend, confidant, mother, and the only female who I was really ever close to, whether that seems healthy or not. Second, I was still a shy, introverted, young woman who wanted to please everyone but was alone. There were so many unanswered questions my mom and I had never talked about—marriage, kids, life! I was truly lonely, and loneliness had come in a big way.

I clearly remember, one evening, saying to myself (Yes, I tend to talk to myself) that I had to make a choice. I could either stay home on a weekday or weekend night alone with no purpose in mind, or I could just put myself out there. I was a *big* girl and could control any situation. I could choose what to drink and how much. I could choose to stay or to leave. I could maybe learn to socialize. What harm would come if I went out, listened to music, went dancing, or just went to a bar. After all, one of my favorite things in the world to do is people watch. I love to watch people's behavior in various settings. So what harm would come if I went out, listened to music, went dancing, or just went to a bar? Third, there was the guilt. Was I totally selfish for moving to Cleveland instead of staying in New York? Had my mother known something I hadn't? If she had, why in the hell hadn't she shared it with me? I shouldn't try to second-guess her thoughts, and it is certainly time to relinquish any and all of the guilt.

I created a guarded place in my heart where I could protect myself from dealing with the loss of my mother and friend as well as the regret of feeling selfish for

◇

leaving New York to do my own thing. The rational side of me said that I was supposed to go find myself and do my own thing. It was my time. Doing it didn't mean I was selfish. However, it was a lot for a twenty-one-year-old to process.

Over time, I learned how to carry that loss and realized that I would not be who I am today and would not be doing what I do if there had been a different outcome. Maybe that is how I have justified my life, but I do believe these experiences carried a lot of value in making me the person that I am.

I took a couple weeks off but then went back to Cleveland like I was supposed to. When I returned there, I was truly alone—lonely and alone. Depression came in like a hurricane, so I sought help. It didn't really do anything for me, so I immersed myself in the genetics laboratory, working with my genetic research and thesis project. When I wasn't in the lab, I became a workout fanatic. I joined a health club, and that became my go to place. I did get in great shape but also used it as a hideaway.

I think the hardest thing to come to terms with was not being able to call and speak to my mother. For anyone who has lost a loved one that is one of the biggest challenges especially if you are used to speaking to that person everyday. Many times, without even thinking about it, you go to pick up the phone to call. It takes time to get over that despair.

I realized I would miss all those adult moments and

◇

my questions would never have answers. There are times I still long for her presence, however as I have aged, I am more energized by my mother's memory. I wish that she was around to see her grandchildren, but I do feel a certain presence and hopefulness that she is watching over them.

Life Stage #3

The Young Adult Stage

(Age Twenty-One to Twenty-Five)

While in graduate school, I met my future husband, whom, strangely enough, I had met before in high school. It's a crazy story, but our parents knew each other. No, it was not an arranged marriage. We had gone out twice and then hadn't spoken to each other for six years. We will get into relationships later, but let me just say, there were times that I still never defined who Robin Joy was. Yes, I was absolutely having a blast with this "new" man in my life, however was unsure about me. It was almost like being two totally different people. The outgoing Robin Joy with her beau and then Robin Joy who was uncomfortable alone by herself. Finding who you are and being comfortable with that is an important aspect of being alone but not lonely.

My family was broken while his was accepting. I guess I found some sense of acceptance and belonging from them. Here's the catch: I was still lonely and a little lost because I didn't really know who I was, in spite of, outside looking in, seemingly having it all together.

I was living in Cleveland, finishing my master's degree in molecular biology and genetics, and teaching classes. My fiancé was living in the Washington DC area after relocating from Philadelphia for work. When I graduated with my master's degree, I kept an apartment near him because my life completely revolved around him. I was in love and lust and was desperate to have this relationship. I guess you can say that I was madly and blindly in love, but I still did not know who I was.

I know that if I hadn't pushed or followed my fiancé, we may not have married. Again, I loved him and chose without regret to be with him as he chose me too. However, if I really look back and analyze the progression of our relationship, I can see how desperate I was for a safe, loving environment. I yearned for someone to love and take care of me. I didn't know who I was and never really gave myself an opportunity to ask, who am I?

So what was my next move? Well I followed the guy, of course. I did what I tell my own daughter and every young woman never to do. I followed my serious boyfriend, at the time, to the Washington DC area and sort of moved in with him.

I strategize and empower my younger clientele by telling them that these are their years to travel, to explore, and to find themselves. The earlier you learn the skills to do that, the less likely you will be to soul search later in life. Now, I am not suggesting that you stop learning and growing. Find what makes you happy and never be afraid of change. Change, especially when

◇

there is a little bit of fear associated with it, is a good, powerful, and exciting thing. Change is growth, and that is always a good thing.

I had never let my "little" Robin grow up and dream. My dreams had been what I had thought others wanted them to be. That was unhealthy and through the years, led to my loneliness and depression.

***

There is an important point that I want to share and encourage all of you to learn from. As you read through these stages described, pause and use this opportunity to reflect on the stages in your own life. Are there times or places where you wanted to please others instead of yourself or where you were afraid? When I looked at those three stages, I realized I was always afraid during my childhood. I was afraid in high school, college, and even into my adult years. I didn't know what I wanted, and my dreams were what I thought others wanted them to be. This was a time full of self-doubt as well as a lack of self-esteem and confidence in myself.

***

When I remember this time, I don't think that I ever gave myself time for self-reflection. I was checking off the boxes on the list that I thought I needed to. Again, absolutely no regrets, but it wasn't until I decided to answer the question, who am I? that I focused on what I was passionate about and truly looked at what made

⬦

me, and only me, happy. Then I was able to feel fully comfortable with my life and myself.

When this took place, the years of my personal struggles with loneliness, depression, and self-doubt came to a screeching halt. That is when I embraced my joys, gifts, and being alone as a positive, happy, comfortable thing. That is when I realized the only race I should be running was my own race and at my own pace.

Fear is normal when you are a young child, however, I never grew out of it. I didn't even realize how negative that lifestyle was. So the *new* me graduated and made a change.

Life Stage #4

Adult Children

(Age Twenty-Six to Fifty-Three)

This stage of life was my life story as I began motherhood. I think all mothers will be able to relate to this particular crossroads, and certainly those of you who are adult women who are single, married without children, divorced, widowed, or may have lost a child faced your own challenging crossroads as you grew into womanhood.

Soon after I was married at twenty-six, I became pregnant and rolled into motherhood. Let me just say this: I love, love, love being a mother. For those of you who are mothers, I hope you have the same joy. For those of you who want to be mothers, no job is harder

⬦

or more rewarding. However, like any job, it takes over your life. There is no handbook for this job. As any mother will tell you, it is easy to lose your sense of self and your identity. It is easy to totally wrap yourself around your child and his or her life.

It is so important to find your passion. It can be anything you like to do, but always find time to dabble in it. If you don't have a passion, find *me* time and explore different things. Reach outside your comfort zone and try something new. It doesn't matter whether your children are young or old. You must carve out time for yourself at every stage of motherhood!

Personally, that is where I failed. I did not keep my own activities going, not that I didn't love what I was doing, but I solely focused my life on my family. My activities were my children's activities. I became a volunteer, driver, and social director. I don't regret this, but even my social life revolved around theirs.

I also want to mention that the family structure I had come from no longer existed. My father and brothers were not involved in my life or the lives of my children. I basically felt like an orphan, which only triggered those feeling of isolation as a younger child, so I was very protective of my own family's structure. In hindsight that is probably why I solely focused on raising my children when they were young almost as a protective response.

My career path revolved around my children's schedules. I had taken several part-time jobs so that I would be available, at the end of the day, for my children. I would never change that part of my life because it was incredibly important to be home, especially as my kids grew older and entered high school. Let me just say that some of my best, most important conversations occurred with my daughter between 11:30 p.m. and 12:00 a.m.

As my children grew older and I could see their college tuitions on the horizon, I went back to salaried office work. I started as a documentation specialist, moved up to training specialist, and then went to a nonprofit organization as a director of education. I was excited because, I was tied to education. I had always enjoyed learning and teaching, so now I was back creating programs for middle school students.

It was a very cool program but brutal at the same time. It consisted of incredibly long hours and was demanding both physically and mentally. The money was good, but I was underpaid for my work. However, the benefits, including health insurance for my family, were great. That made my husband happy because he didn't have those benefits.

However, the dark side was that I was in a downward spiral. Not only was I exhausted but the company's work environment was completely emotionally unhealthy. I was beat down by an abusive boss. Although I could stand in front of an entire school of students and administrators while delivering a powerful presentation, when my boss was present, I completely regressed and felt suppressed.

My boss had her own darkness. She was dealing with unhappiness. Some people are just like that. They try

◇

to deal with their unhappiness by making others look bad so they can look good. She had her own insecurities.

Unfortunately, her verbal abuse exhausted me. It was such an unhealthy environment that my depression ramped up like it had when I was back in Cleveland after the loss of my mother. I don't like admitting this, but as I stated earlier, I am going to be completely real, honest, and authentic. So here I go. Several times (maybe more than several), I drove down the road while trying to figure out the best way to take my own life. I wondered, *If I drive off this one ramp near my house, will that be efficient enough?* I only wanted to hurt myself.

It was a very dark time for me. I was on depression medication although I was embarrassed to admit that I had depression. Some days were much harder than others were. My own self-sabotaging voices screamed so loudly, I felt everyone would be better off if I was gone. I figured that my husband and my boys would be fine. I truly thought they would, but then there was my daughter.

I didn't want my girl, who was my best friend, to go through her adult life without her mother. How could I do this to her? After all, I knew how hard it was to lose a mother at a young age, and she was even younger than I had been. Who would talk to her about all the topics I wished I had a chance to talk to my own mother about. I knew I had to pull myself up out of that deep, dark, lonely, cold well. I was better than what those voices told me I was. I was worth more, and nothing was going to take away my chance to watch my daughter grow and enter her adult years.

Soon after that, I walked into my office and announced my resignation. I decided to launch my own business because I never again wanted anyone to make me feel trapped and causing me to regress back to feeling like that five year old child living in fear. Financially, the decision may have been rash. I know my husband wished I had stayed until I had had a better business plan, however, for my own well-being, I couldn't stay any longer.

Up to this point I had gone through life hiding my struggles well. It was something I was good at, and I don't think even my husband knew how much I was struggling. Interestingly though, my daughter was the first to comment, after I had been gone from that job two or three months, how different I seemed. I wasn't angry or sad. I seemed lighter and happier. She was quite intuitive and always had been.

From that moment forward, I took steps to transform who I was and to listen to myself. It still took another few years until I became certified as a teen coach. Several certifications followed this, such as a Mindfulness-Based Stress Reduction, Transformational Leader, and Women's Empowerment. I finally knew what I wanted to do when I grew up. For the first time, I didn't ask permission to do it. In fact, I didn't even ask my husband his thoughts or if he minded that I was spending money on it. I just did it, and I did it for me.

Between the ages of forty-eight and fifty-three, it was my time to find me. I was tired of playing by everyone else's rules and asked myself, *When did I stop being me and letting my own opinion matter?* I bring this up for a few reasons and want to make a distinction for the reader. First, I was the mother of three adult children. All of my kids were home from their respective locations for the holidays. I had shopped, cooked, etc., and came home to three kids on the couch and two sinks filled with dirty dishes. Their first question to me was, "Did you pick up food for lunch." This triggered the following response, as you can imagine: "You are twenty, twenty-two, and twenty-five. Get you're a**** up." It had been like three little kids yelling, "Mom, Mom!"

It made me furious, but it was also a wake-up call for me. Even though I felt like I had launched my independence, I also felt like I had taken a few steps backward and lost my balance. It was almost as if I had had to find my inner voice, assert myself and reintroduce myself as the new version of me. However, the real question is did I enable this behavior?

Anyway, I loved and still love helping people but have learned to stop volunteering for everything. I have learned that if it doesn't feel right or if someone isn't genuine, I don't have the time to associate with that individual.

If you begin to watch people, you will be surprised how many are not authentic, which brings up a couple of things. First, be authentic and be with people who are real. Your true friends will be supportive and encouraging. Second, although this is truly a hard habit to break, stop saying yes to everything. We will get back to this, but choose wisely in life. You have the right and need to prioritize you first. If you are not healthy and in alignment, you will not be your best for anyone or anything else, including your family or career.

***

This is a really important lesson and tip of the day. Many women do not learn this and freak out when they become empty nesters. Ladies, life is tough, and the best gift you can give your children is to let them know that life is tough. We make mistakes, but it is from our mistakes that we grow stronger and learn. It is an important lesson in resilience, which, frankly, our children and society need to learn more about.

When did you lose your identity? You didn't and shouldn't either. Just because you have the role of mother, which lasts forever, of course, that doesn't mean you can't have a passion that is yours alone. Relish it and keep it sacred. Not everything needs to be shared. It is also okay not to fix everything. We always try. That's just in our DNA. However, the one lesson that can be most valuable for us as well as our children is to accept is that all people fall down. You get back up and find another way to try again. This builds resilience and strength.

◇

That's my story. Now let's talk about yours. Whether you are single, married with or without children, divorced, or widowed, here is a point you need to be conscious of. Be aware of behaviors that signal past habits or patterns you are trying to change or break. The more you recognize these behaviors, the less likely you are to give into the habits and patterns of the past.

***

CHAPTER 2

Discovering Your Path

Understanding the difference between alone, loneliness, and being lonely, will both negatively and positively help you understand the triggers and transformation that is necessary to deal with the connotations of each word. Alone is just that. This is when you are by yourself, either physically or mentally. Loneliness can be twofold. First, there is the loneliness that refers to isolation, which is usually not a choice and is lonely. Secondly, there is the loneliness that relates solitude. In that sense, loneliness isn't lonely and can be a choice as well as life-giving. Knowing and understanding these triggers will help clarify and identify past patterns and assist you in consciously deciding to break patterns and to move forward. These actions will help you break any destructive cycles.

As I approached my fifty-third birthday on August 11, 2017, I realized that I was at my own personal crossroads. It was a very weird feeling because that had been when my mother had passed away. As I have said, I didn't view the fifties as old anymore. This was probably because I was in my fifties, but nonetheless I didn't feel old. By the way, what should old feel like?

Over the last several years, I had so much heaviness in my life. Most of this heaviness centered on money, which was never my favorite subject anyway. Starting and growing my own business, along with college tuitions, as well as my husband's business going through its own changes, everything seemed to revolve around money.

For a while, I thought if I could take care of the pressures that money brought and try to handle it all alone, which meant keeping it to myself, the burden would be only on my shoulders. Why did I think this way? Well, possibly my own self-sabotaging voices reminding me of my self-destructive feelings as well as protecting everyone else. In my mind I was protecting my family by alleviating any stress for them while increasing stress of my own. All that accomplished was that it caused me to revert into a dark mind-set, which I was working so hard to get out of. I consciously chose this mind-set. I was the only one who could control

◇

either a downward or upward spiral. Not that it was easy, but it was my choice.

Money was one of those *bad* words in my vocabulary and had been my entire life. It wasn't only an issue in my marriage but had been one throughout my childhood. In order for me to change, I needed to break the cycle. My personal relationship with money was an unhealthy relationship, and I had made a conscious decision that the next fifty years were going to be filled with only healthy relationships and mind-sets.

Although money had been one of the most difficult hurdles in my marriage—almost to the breaking point— it was a hurdle that I had brought into the marriage as baggage. My husband and I could make poor financial decisions on our own, however, the way that I handled our conversations or lack of those conversations was a direct result of how I had dealt with the issue in my younger years.

All I really wanted to do was start over. Obviously, I would keep my kids but my marriage was on edge. I wanted to shed everything. However, the more I thought about that, the more I realized I had better really think about what I wanted to do for me. What would make me the happiest? My mission was to do some soul-searching so I could understand and define Robin Joy Meyers as an individual. That was really the key. I was ready to focus on my true happiness and self-worth. I was ready to feel alive rather than just be alive.

The point is that we very often deal with situations

◇

in the moment without reflecting on any past patterns. You may be dealing with the marital issue of communication, which is causing a breakdown in your relationship, but my suggestion is that you take time to reflect and see if this issue is a similar pattern from your past. If you are able to identify, acknowledge, and bring closure to that pattern, then it is easier to move on and break any cycle. Otherwise, you never really have full closure on the situation.

In order to move on and truly be happy, fulfilled, and aligned, we need to claim our most honest, authentic selves and allow ourselves second, third, or fourth chances to truly be happy. That is when we are our most powerful selves. Again, this is all about self-growth. There should be no regrets but only reclaiming you.

***

On a side note, I went through my days as an overall happy and productive person, but there were certainly those days when my own negative, self-sabotaging voices handcuffed me. I fell back into the young Robin. Ironically, I am a very optimistic person and always have been. However, using some of the strategies discussed later in chapter five, I began my transformational journey to discovering who Robin Joy Meyers was truly meant to be.

***

CHAPTER 3

Commit to Your Vision

The Three Cs of Life

You must make a *CHOICE* to take a *CHANCE* to make a *CHANGE*. I want to share with you how I made this conscious commitment as I began my own transition. Not only was I coaching on this subject matter but was also undergoing my own personal transformation. It really does begin with the subconscious mind.

Choice

What I have always believed in and coached on has been based on how I could serve others. I asked my clients to get out of their own way, so it was time for me to commit to this too, by making my own changes. In order to do that I first had to align my subconscious and conscious minds, which all came down to the word *mind-set*. Mind-set is a way of thinking and a set of beliefs that can determine someone's actions. According to The Free Dictionary, mind-set is defined as "a fixed mental attitude or disposition that predetermines a person's responses to and interpretations of situations; an inclination or a habit" (www.thefreedictionary.com/mindset). If we change those beliefs into positive ones, our mind-set can be more positive and, therefore, more powerful.

Chance

I realized that my transformation was like hitting the reset button. As my vision freed me of past life stages and I let go of my fears, I began to create a lighter, happier, more fulfilling lifestyle. I became more confident and started taking *me* time every day. The interesting and best part is that as I began to show up more for myself, I showed up more for my family, friends, colleagues, and clients. I started to attract more clients than ever and really felt in control of me.

I still had days when my own self-sabotaging voices were in my head. However, those voices have become less and less frequent over time. When they have raised their unwelcome volume, I have used several techniques such as breathing, meditation, or

◇

a five-second rule, which I will discuss more in the next part of this book. I have learned to recognize the triggers and, coincidentally, have learned to overcome them more efficiently every day.

Change

The result is that I have changed. I have changed my way of thinking and how to put things in a better perspective. I have learned to find time in each and every day to stop, think, and breathe. I think about the day ahead and set my intentions. I remember why I am grateful. Overall, I am a stronger, happier, healthier version of me, who is now turning fifty-three, than I ever was.

I have learned it is never too late to create the life you want to have. Don't waste time because you deserve more. You have earned it! You should appreciate and value your life as well as guard your precious time.

***

Those who don't respect this new side of you should not be in your chosen circle. Surround yourself by your chosen team—those whom you fully trust, who are authentic, and who will be there to guide and support you no matter what. Sometimes that can be a family member or a close friend. Remember that no one should make you feel like you are less so he or she can look better at your expense.

PART 2

Theory

The Practicality of Getting in Action

In part two of this book, I would like to teach you the most effective tools to unblocking your blocks; reclaiming your identity; and being unapologetically you. Part of getting in action is being ready and acknowledging that you want to transform. As many of my clients and I have discussed, one has to be ready to move forward. In order to accept these transitions, it really comes down to one thing: your personal alignment. What is your personal alignment you may ask? By definition, "a persons alignment is represents their general outlook and approach to life" (The Social

Psychology of Alignment). If your personal alignment is happy and satisfied, you have the key to success. If you are aligned with yourself, it will spread into your happiness with your personal and professional life and result in a work/life balance.

CHAPTER 4

Unblocking
Your Blocks

As a life strategist, my motto is as follows: "Unblock your blocks so your life rocks." What are these blocks? Honestly, many, if not most, of these blocks are our own self-induced thoughts and insecurities. Often these thoughts and insecurities can be self-inflicted or from years of past behaviors, we have or have not had control of.

For example, if you are told from a young age that you are not as talented as your sibling is, you become quite insecure. It's no wonder that you have self-doubt. Sometimes we are able to brush it off, but often, we are not able to suppress the thoughts. Sometimes these thoughts can be so crippling they can prevent us from getting out of bed and being productive.

Why is it so easy to sabotage ourselves? Usually, we are our own worst enemy. We allow those little voices inside our heads to sabotage our good, positive thoughts. I always think of the image of the good conscious sitting on one shoulder while the bad conscious sits on the other. Don't let anyone fool you because you are not alone. Everyone has those conflicting, negative thoughts sometimes. The key is what you do to handle these thoughts. How do you overcome them and shut them down? How do you become the most powerful you?

The first thing we all forget to do is treat ourselves just like we treat our best friends. Why can we be so real, gentle, loving, and authentic with our best friends but so critical and impatient with ourselves?

What if you were to change your way of thinking and speaking to yourself ? Instead of letting these negative, self-sabotaging voices take over, let them empower you. These voices can still offer productive criticism, but there is a different way to say them. Do you remember your childhood? I am sure you were told the same as I was, "If you don't have anything nice to say, then don't say it at all."

Think about the idea of you being your own best friend. You might be wondering why. Well, it is because you treat your best friend with patience and encouragement. If you are like me, you are there for

◇

your best friend whether she needs you to listen and give advice or just let her debrief and rant over a situation. You are honest and a true advocate, only wanting the best for your friend. You cheer the successes that come his or her way or are a shoulder when your friend needs a good cry.

I have a another question for you: Why can't you treat yourself the same way you treat your best friend? Why can't you listen, encourage, cheer yourself on, and give yourself a pat on the back when things don't go the way you want them to? Why can't you lend yourself a hand, pick yourself up, and set yourself back on your feet again?

Again, here is the advice that I want you to take away from this chapter: Treat yourself like you are your best friend. Speak to yourself just like you speak to your best friend. Does this sound easy? Well, it's not that easy because we tend to be our toughest critic.

Please refer to chapter 6 for some strategies. An example would be the five-second rule. Take five seconds before you respond and remind yourself that you are strong. As you begin to practice these tools, you will see a shift in yourself and your mind-set. This takes practice. It's just like training a new muscle, so repetition is necessary.

***

On a side note: As you enter this phase of unblocking your blocks, remember that you need to acknowledge

◇

the past—put closure to it and move on. You need to find healing no matter what the circumstances are. For example, if you are dealing with or have dealt with loss, it can be devastating. However, in order to transform yourself and move forward, you must allow yourself to go through the grieving process, therefore allowing closure and peace. Let me preface this by saying it is not as easy as it sounds. There are different kinds of loss, and the idea of moving past something is often not possible. This is especially true when the loss is great, which all losses are. So in order to move forward, learn to hold a space for that loss until you are strong enough to carry it. Slowly, the loss will become part of your new reality.

A beneficial exercise for you would be to write down what you would say to your best friend if he or she was not able to do something or had no value. In a sense, you are playing a role reversal. It gives you the opportunity to see how you would react to the situation. Then compare what you have written to how you would want your friend to respond to you in the same situation so you could see the difference. These conscious steps will allow you to break the cycle and to play and dream bigger as you create the life that you want!

***

CHAPTER 5

A New Way to Think

Now that you have made the commitment to unblock your blocks so your life rocks, let's create a systematic way of thinking that will allow you to begin your transformation. Let's break this chapter into three steps: "Identifying Your Circle of Influence," "Relationships Got a Hold on You," and "Your Personal Message." So ready, set, go!

Step 1

Identifying Your Circle of Influence

◇

The first step in identifying your circle of influence is finding and relying on your support staff. This is the safety net, group, or tribe you trust and relate to. You need to build your own personal circle of influence that you feel totally supported by.

When trying to discern the relationships that you will create this circle from, choose people who will support and believe in you and with whom you can be your true authentic self. Sometimes that might be a large group, and other times, it may only be a small handful of people.

My team is just a handful of people and may seem small; however, it has my back. These people are strong, powerful beings I can lean on for anything.

Allow your team members, no matter how small, to have your back and to support you through whatever life transitions you are facing. Be open and accepting of their presence because they are there to acknowledge you in whatever capacity you may need them to. These are your peeps, so don't try to do it by yourself. Lean on other people the same way you would support them.

Step 2

Relationships Got a Hold on You

Another important aspect to consider when you are ready to put your systems in place is your relationship

◇

with people who are in or were in your life. This bold move will happen as you are transformed and allow yourself to be satisfied with being alone and no longer lonely.

Some of these people may include family members. Remember that you cannot choose your family. I hope you like your family members as well as love them. But not everyone has that dynamic or support system form their family so look to those you are closest to and those relationships that give you the most joy and support.

Although this sounds difficult, finding your alignment and your "alone but not lonely" time comes down to the ability to let go. Let go of the things you cannot control as well as those that weigh you down. For example, an unhealthy relationship is an abusive relationship. No one should make you feel bad about yourself or less of a person for any reason.

If you go back to chapter one, you can reread the section about poor relationships. Unhealthy relationships often come with friendships. Those can be ever changing.

When you have children, many of your friendships revolve around your children's activities. As I know from personal experience, friendships with parents can sometimes be strained when your children are having problems with those parents' kids. From experience do not force your adult friendships on your children and vice versa. There a distinction between friendships and social acquaintances, so when choosing your support team and your children are involved, keep your adult friendship separate from your child's friendship.

The positive side of relationships is when you rekindle long lost friendships of the past. I have rekindled some of my relationships from college, which I am so thankful for. One, in particular, has truly made a significant difference in my life. It has been fun to see where our lives are at now. This all becomes a piece in the overall puzzle.

Surround yourself with like-minded people who empower you, have a similar mind-set, challenge you in a positive ways, and whom you enjoy being around. These are your peeps, cheerleaders, advocates, or tribe members. Whatever you want to call them, this is group has your back. They will support you through your transformation as you transition to your most powerful self.

Be open to these transitions because change is good and positive. So often, we, as a society, look at change as a negative failure. Well, let me be the first to tell you that you can use these transitions as an opportunity to move forward. Don't look at change from a fear-based, negative perspective. It is a step forward to something else. Remember, the end goal is you being confident and unapologetically you.

◇

Step 3

Your Personal Message

Finally, record a message to yourself that makes you feel powerful. Your message should remind you that you are strong and unstoppable. Any time you feel self-doubt, play this message for yourself. You can play it when you are driving to an important meeting or are having one of those days when you don't feel your best.

If you want to go a step further, pick a favorite song that makes you feel good, empowered, and strong. My favorite go-to song is by Idina Menzel and is called, "Queen of Swords." I play this on my way to meetings, events, or speaking engagements. It makes me feel good, confident, and unapologetically me.

***

Right here begin your own transformation with these three steps. Use the rest of this piece of paper to begin a list of who is in your tribe. Name one to three people who have your back anytime day or night. Next, take a moment to reflect on your relationships. Are there any particular relationships that are weighing you down? Maybe it is time to have a conversation with that person. Finally, before you take a step further I want you to pick your most powerful song that you just love to sing out loud. The song that makes you feel strong, powerful, confident and unstoppable. Write

◇

that song down here and then download that song on your iPhone or android as soon as possible. Also take a voice memo of you telling yourself why you are strong, powerful, confident and unstoppable. This is for you to hear only so speak from the heart and no retakes. This is about being real not perfect. Whenever I have one of those days that I do not feel at my best, I play my 20 seconds of "me." It makes me feel good and ready to go. Trust me and try it!

***

CHAPTER 6

Specific Strategies to Change Your Life

Because there are different areas we may have to address as we change our lives, there are also different strategies to help us achieve our goals. The following strategies cover our minds and spirits and were developed throughout the years. While working as a life strategist, here are several of my favorite strategies, which you can implement immediately.

I want to warn you that you will be training a new muscle if you have never used any of these strategies. As with anything new, practice makes perfect. I suggest that you choose one or two of these strategies at a time.

◇

Practice and get consistent in your use of them and then add in another new strategy.

Why do we second-guess our strengths? Why can't we say, "Thank you," to a compliment without giving a whole explanation as to the meaning of that compliment? Why? Why? Why? Honestly, I have no idea why! It is something in the female mind-set. We are brought up with it, but I am here to say enough is enough. It is time, no matter how old or young you are, to make that change. It is time to put you first. No, that is not being a bitch, as some would say. It is being a woman who believes in herself and is confident, comfortable, and aligned with her own being. She is willing to ask for something. What's the worst thing that can happen? Someone might say *no*!

Mind-Set

The first element to mind-set is the quieting of your mind. If you do not make an effort to quiet your mind from useless, loud, and unnecessary thoughts, you will become overloaded and exhausted. However, when you fill your mind with positive thoughts, your mind will become a powerful engine that can jump-start change. In other words, your mind-set can dictate your results and the ability to make a change. So if you have an old model of mind-set, it is time for an upgrade.

Mind-set is how you talk to yourself. Changing your mind-set is a process and takes practice. For example, when you transitioned from riding a tricycle to a bicycle, you had to learn to balance differently. You had to learn this balance before it became a habit. This habit is what becomes a new process.

To simplify the discussion, I will break the process into a proven three-step formula. The three steps are as follows: "Dream It," "Believe It," and "Put It in Action."

Dream It

The first step is to dream bigger. Create the vision you want to achieve. We have talked about making an upgrade, and that is exactly what you are doing.

Believe It

The second step is a little more difficult because you have to let go of your fears and existing beliefs, which include those self-sabotaging little voices. It is vital, in this step, to pinpoint the misalignment between your conscious and subconscious, which often deals with your self-image. Here you will deprogram past negatives and reprogram the belief that you are good enough. Let go of self-doubt and what others may think of you. This relates to your personal and professional lives.

◇

Put It in Action

Once you have shifted your beliefs, you are ready to commit to your vision and to put your plan in action. This is the final step where you will shift your mind-set beyond the self-doubt, self-sabotage, and procrastination and into the strong, confident, capable, resilient, and courageous person you know you are. The moment you shift your mind-set, your life changes for the better. Now you are playing big in your game of life.

Lighten Your Load

Anyone who claims he or she can multitask can admit to this. How many times have you offered to volunteer or join just one more committee because help is needed, especially when you have children? In one sense, it is great, because you get to be part of your child's world. On the other hand, you *cannot* do everything. There are limited hours in a day, and you cannot be effective for anyone if you are spread too thin. Direct your energy at a few great causes rather than too many good causes where you can't be as effective.

When I began my work as a life strategist, I spread myself very thin. It was all for excellent causes. However, a point came where I had to make a decision about where I wanted to spend my time. Therefore, I stepped down from a couple of boards that I had been involved with and turned down a few speaking

◇

engagements. I realized I wasn't as effective as I could be.

If there is an activity or event that you would like to volunteer for, take a day to think about it. You can wait a day and get back to someone. Then consider the five-second rule, which is described next.

The Five-Second Rule

Here is a little secret that I suggest to all of my clients. It's called the five-second rule. It's just like when you were a kid and something dropped on the ground. If you wanted it bad enough, you would still eat it if it had only been on the ground for five seconds.

The five-second rule is an easy concept, which starts today as you read this book. It takes practice, and just like anything else, it's like training a muscle. Every time you start to hear the voices of doubt in your head, count down from five to one. Then remind yourself that you are strong, powerful, and in control of what you want to do. Think of this as your pause and reset button.

Rituals

A ritual can be defined as a sequence of activities or set of actions that helps you get anything you want primarily for its symbolic value. It creates a pattern of repetition. It is a formal behavior that is practiced

◇

consistently just like a tradition. (https://en.wikipedia.org/wiki/Ritual)

I will break these into morning and evening rituals. You need to start slowly and try not to feel overwhelmed. Remember that habits are like muscles, so you are in training.

Morning

How do you care for yourself in the morning so that you will be your most radiant and aligned self? The most vital, strategic step for a successful life begins with your morning routine. It is imperative to begin your day with clarity and intention. No matter what stage of life you are in, I cannot stress enough that these morning rituals need to begin today.

You may only have five minutes, but when you see the improvement in the start your day, you will want to increase that time. I started with five minutes a day. I already get up very early, and it wasn't easy. Again, you are retraining the way you think, so before you decide against doing these exercises, you need to try these new behaviors for at least one week.

Wake up and find a quiet place. When my children lived at home, my place was my closet. I could shut the door and not wake anyone up. First, I would stretch, whether it was a set of simple stretches or a series of Pilates/Yoga exercises to start my blood flowing.

Next, hydration is very important. Drink a tall

◇

glass of water, sit quietly, and enjoy the silence. If you enjoy meditation, this is the perfect time. I have done as little as a three-minute guided meditation. There are great apps and recordings that can help. Whatever you choose to do, the idea is to calm your mind and to quiet the noise. Find your inner zen.

After doing that, begin to visualize what you want from your day. Set your intentions and if needed, be prepared to reward yourself at the end of the day when you have achieved your goals. Be careful here though. This is not a honey-do list. This is seeing what would make your day as a success.

While doing your visualizations, talk to yourself gently, just like you are speaking to your best friend. Give yourself affirmations, which are positive, encouraging words about you. Take some time to write. Keep a small journal nearby where you can write down your thoughts. This will not only allow you to process your thoughts but also help you become more aware of your true self.

If you can only do two exercises, label one page with the word *gratitude* and the other with *affirmations*. Every morning, try to add something to each of those pages. What are you grateful for? It can be as simple as waking up to start a new day. Affirmations are words that describe your powerful self. They can be adjectives such as strong, powerful, passionate, or unstoppable.

***

Again, you are training a new muscle. These habits are not going to feel natural or happen overnight. It will take a concerted effort to spend two to three minutes each morning by yourself, quietly to doing this exercise. At first, you may feel you have no words or they may seem repetitive. That is perfectly okay. Your level of comfort will grow, and you will see a difference.

***

Evening

In my opinion, your evening ritual will be a little more challenging and will take discipline and training. Decide whether or not you can sustain this routine every night or if it needs to be a weekend event when you have more time.

When my children were still at home, it didn't matter whether they were little ones or in high school. Sometimes their activities ended late, by the time they went to bed, I was asleep on the floor. So I suggest that you do what works for you.

The evening work is not difficult but is as follows: At the end of your day, try to allow ten-to-fifteen minutes for this activity. Disconnect from the world. That means no more phone, television, or social media. You only need your pen and journal.

Write down three things that made you happy that day. These can be anything, such as people, tasks, and

◇

accomplishments. Do not dwell on what you didn't finish that day. The reason is this: When you go to bed with a positive mind-set, you clear your mind. There is scientific proof that you will have a better night's sleep.

Meditation

Meditation comes in many forms and can be personalized to your liking. Some people can meditate in a room full of people while others, like myself, cannot relax enough or relax too much.

Let me share a story. I attended a one-day workshop, which a friend of mine was facilitating. The meditation portion had come, so we all had our yoga mats. You could lie down or sit up—whichever made you more comfortable.

I am usually not comfortable in these situations. I close my eyes but then start peeking too see if everyone has his or her eyes closed. I find it hard to relax.

However, the facilitator read through the meditation, and in a matter of minutes, I was totally out like a light. The good news is that my daughter woke me up before I began snoring loudly.

If you do not like group meditation, practice it on your own. If you don't follow a specific person or track, use this time to sit quietly and be still. If you would like to, add music to this time that is soothing.

Whether you are a spiritual person or not, find a quiet place where you can close your eyes and focus on the quietness. Practice deep breathing for three-to-five minutes. If you enjoy meditation, there are some wonderful apps you can subscribe too. I find that meditation is a personal thing, and you need to make this work for you. Adapt it accordingly to your comfort level.

Bullet Journaling

For as long as I can remember, I have loved keeping journals. I usually keep several, which includes the ones I write in, a calendar, daily logs, and so on.

Within the last year, I have become very passionate about the bullet journaling technique. I am certainly not the founder of it or the first to use it. What I love about it is you can personalize it to your needs.

Bullet journaling is a wonderful way to keep your calendar together with your thoughts. There are plenty of people who use bullet journaling, and in fact, a business has grown from it. You can order a specific bullet journal at www.bulletjournal.com, however, I just bought a plain notebook at Target. It really is a personal preference. I like lined paper. Individuals I have shared this technique with have personally styled notebooks.

Look at the bullet journal as a framework. This framework consists of modules. Modules are methods designed to help collect and organize specific kinds of entries. The power of the bullet journal is that you can mix and match these modules to best suit your needs.

◇

Let's take a look at the four core modules: *index, daily log, monthly log,* and *quarterly log.*

Index

The first few pages of the journal are your index. The index is where the bullet journal really comes together. As you start to use your journal, simply add the topics of your collections and their page numbers to the index so you can quickly find and reference them at any point.

Daily Log

The daily log is designed for day-to-day use. At the top of the page, record the date as your topic. Throughout the course of the day, simply rapid log your tasks, events, and notes as they occur. If you don't fill the page, add the next date wherever you left off, and you're ready to continue.

Monthly Log

The monthly log helps you organize—you guessed it— your month. It consists of a calendar and a task list. To set up your first monthly log, go to the next available spread of facing pages. The left page will be your calendar, and the right will be your task page. The calendar gives you a bird's-eye view of the month.

◇

To set it up, write the current month's name at the top of the page. Now list all the dates of that month down the left margin followed by the first letter of the corresponding day.

Quarterly Log

Set up your quarterly log by drawing lines for a six-month calendar. You'll need to draw two equally-spaced, horizontal lines across facing pages. Do this to four pages. My advice would be to keep the calendar on the left and major monthly events on the right. Set aside a few separate pages to write down what you are grateful for, your daily affirmations, and/or words that make you feel powerful.

Creating Your Journal

The best way to begin is to buy a five-by-eight- or six-by-nine-inch notebook/journal with lined paper. My journal has about ninety pages.

Set up an index of your sections. I leave five extra pages per section. That way if I want to add anything, I will have room to do so. Leave a few pages for gratitude, daily affirmations, and a calendar section, which I separated into two sections.

The first calendar section is divided into a quarterly format. Divide the page into thirds. You will need four

◇

pages since there are four quarters in a year and three months per quarter.

Devote one full page per month to the second calendar section. You will need twelve pages. Each page line will represent one day.

What you do with the rest of the journal is up to you. The beauty of the bullet journal is that you can customize it solely for you. My journal includes sections for this book, my clients, events, and my year's goals.

What I love about the bullet journal is that everything is in one place. Even though I have an iPhone, my journal travels everywhere with me. Many people ask me whether they should use a pencil or pen? I personally like to use a pencil. This is important as you get used to this new process.

***

Here is a side note: All these tools need to work for you and take time to adapt to. They may feel awkward and uncomfortable at times, but I guarantee that you will see a change in your life. Please put forth the effort to use the tools you choose for at least one week if not two. As you get comfortable with that one particular tool, add another one into your day.

If your life is anything like mine, I want to give you a little heads-up. Making these changes is important for you to do. You will see a shift in your alignment and your life. You will also be able to acknowledge that you have and are changing. So will your family and friends.

◇

Some people will accept these changes with ease while others may be a little shocked. It rattled my household for a short while, but now I think my family likes this new and improved version of myself. I show up happier, am present, and have given my children, especially my daughter, the tools to learn these behaviors earlier in life. Here's the thing. I *have* changed, and this *is* me—the true, authentic, unapologetic me. Everyone else just has to get used to it. That feels really great to say!

***

PART 3

Making It Personal

(Trials and Tribulations)

As I started the journey of writing this book, it was my goal to ask as many people as possible what being alone but not lonely meant to them. I will be sharing their answers and stories with you because you may be able to relate to them. Although you may not directly see yourselves fitting into each of these stories, I hope that you will be able to apply even a portion of these stories to your own lives.

CHAPTER 7

Stories about Relationships (Its My Turn Now)

Family

Family relationships are one of the trickiest to maneuver. Back in chapter 5, I mentioned that there is a difference between loving a person in your bloodline and liking that person. Sometimes we may love someone but don't necessarily like him or her. The first story is about the journey of deciding to let go of an unhealthy relationship.

◇

Angel

Angel was the youngest of three children and the only girl of the family. Her two older brothers were four and seven years older than she was. Their sibling relationships were rather normal. Typical bickering and finger pointing was common. Angel's relationship with her eldest brother was closer overall, because there was a greater gap in their ages and less commonality to fight over.

As life continued, Angel's brothers focused in their own relationships and lives just as she was focusing on hers. Let's fast-forward to the time when both her parents passed away. This was when the cracks began to appear in their relationships.

First, their mother passed away. Angel was the only one who lived far away from her parents. Her relationship with her brothers became strained. Both of her brothers were older and lived in or near their hometown. Not only did they not communicate with her often but also did not have her back. In fairness, the brothers were handling their own lives as well as dealing with the loss of their mother.

Her brother's wives took certain possessions of Angel's mother's, which should have been passed down to the only daughter of the family. Both wives had living parents and would have similar items passed on to them when the time came. Angel didn't hold onto that baggage. She was, however, disappointed because these

◇

were family items she would never be able to give to her own daughter.

It became a confusing time because Angel lived out of town, had lost her mother, and felt abandoned by her existing family. It wasn't the material objects that really mattered but the sentimental value that was attached to these objects. Figuratively, Angel swept her emotions under the rug and continued to relate to her siblings in the same way. However, the relationships became a little tarnished.

Then Angel and her brothers' father passed away, and the siblings' relationship was going to be tested once again. This added more strain, but this time, Angel was a little more outspoken and present. Angel had not been present when her mother had passed away. She still lived out of state. However, she was now married and raising her family.

One brother was to handle the executorship, which no one quarreled over. When it came time to go through their father's belongings, the siblings all gathered. For the most part, everyone agreed on who was to take which possessions. There were still some petty moments, but Angel was not a fighter. It was just another chapter to be closed.

The year had continued, and the formality of the will was handled. There was not much in the way of an inheritance, however, the brother who was the executor was awarded an amount for his time and effort above and beyond the other two siblings.

Let's continue to fast-forward. Each sibling was raising a family and had reached certain milestones. They all lived in separate states. Angel's daughter actually is residing very close to where her uncle lives, and although Angel's relationship was not any better with her brother, you would hope that he would be available for his niece. Unfortunately, that was not the case which caused any remaining relationship to diminish even further. There was always an underlying negative resentment because of how the past had been handled and due to the lack of communication this began to fester. It festered until, one day, a brother asked Angel to pay for the maintenance on their parents' cemetery plot. The three children had been splitting the cost for several years, but this year was different. It really irked Angel to have to pay this. Financially, Angel was struggling. She wondered if this was going to be a never-ending financial commitment.

Wasn't that resolved through the probate process of the will? Shouldn't her brother have taken care of that? These questions arose until Angel finally decided to ask. As Angel pondered these questions, she felt as if it was time for answers, so she asked. To say that her brother was furious would be an understatement. He had many reasons and explanations but never an answer for Angel.

Angel had had enough and made a decision that day. Yes, she loved her brothers because they were her brothers. If one of them needed her, she would be there to help in any way that she could. However, this relationship had had many strains on it for quite some time.

Even though it may sound sad to the reader, Angel wanted only positive relationships in her life. The relationship with this brother had been a very negative, heavy one for years. There was a time when Angel had asked for help from that brother and he had refused to give it to her. It had been a request that would not have cost him a dime. She had just needed shelter and support for an evening.

So the point that Angel wants you to understand is that relationships are a two-way street. Although this was her brother, she felt that this was a heavy, unhealthy relationship she needed to bring closure to.

Friends

Although this is a story about a friendship, it is much more than that. This story is about overcoming the challenges of a particular friendship and a woman reclaiming her identity so she could find her powerful self without any guilt or apologies. I want to share this story because I know I have lived through this as I think many others also have.

You meet someone and become instant friends. That's what happened when Jordyn met Nancy. Nancy and Jordyn met at a school event several years ago. Jordyn said that they seemed to be instant friends and started to do many things together. They had similar interests. Jordyn probably spent more time with Nancy than with her own husband at times.

Jordyn wasn't an introvert, however, she was soft-spoken, flexible, and easygoing. Sometimes that was misconstrued, but she did have a voice. She didn't always use her voice, but as her relationship with Nancy grew, she felt like she was being smothered. For a while, she thought it was her own insecurity. However, as time went on, she realized that Nancy was insecure.

Although she valued their friendship, she began to lose her identity. Everything and anything that they did was by Nancy's rules, and Jordyn was always busy. She almost felt as if she had another child that she was taking care of.

Slowly she started to find her voice and reclaim the things that she enjoyed. Some of those things included Nancy's company while others did not. Since then, it has become a much healthier and enjoyable relationship.

The strange aspect of this relationship was that Jordyn often wondered if it was her dependency on Nancy or vice versa. However, she learned to find her voice again without feeling guilty. She was allowed to set her boundaries. She was always worried that she might hurt Nancy's feelings but was only hurting herself. Now, when they are together, Jordyn is much more present and engaging.

***

◇

Have you ever experienced a friendship like this? How did you handle it? Often, we don't want to hurt the other one's feelings but that can come at a cost to ourselves. Relationships are very often not equally split fifty percent. Sometimes one side needs a little more support than the other side. However, if a relationship feels unbalanced and unhealthy, then it it not a relationship that you should remain in.

***

Marriage

Let me introduce you to my very dear friend Rebecca. Rebecca is a typical suburban mother, wife, and teacher. For all the years that I have known her, Rebecca has seemed to have it all. All three kids have been happy, have played sports, and have always done very well in school. Her husband was a very successful professional, and life seemed good. It seemed like she had it all, however, appearances can be deceiving. What no one saw was that Rebecca was struggling on the inside.

For most of her marriage and while the kids were young, life went on day by day. Rebecca's world revolved around her kids, their activities, and maintaining her home. She absolutely had no complaints. Rebecca was happy and felt privileged to be able to be a stay-at-home mother. That had been her chosen profession, and she did a magnificent job of it.

◇

However, like many of us women, as Rebecca's children entered young adult life, reality set in. Life had been laser focused around the family until she asked, "Who am I?" Rebecca's older children were twins and only fifteen months older than the third child, so college was approaching at the speed of light.

Rebecca's children had been in high school when she started looking ahead to the future when the kids would leave for college. She had always volunteered at the schools, so she to get a full-time teaching position.

Rebecca wanted more than what her marital relationship was giving her. In fact, she was happiest when she was alone and able to do the things that she loved most, many of which were outdoor activities. As she grew and discovered her passions, she realized how different she was from her husband.

As her two older children prepared to graduate from high school, Rebecca knew that she didn't have a fulfilling marriage. Rebecca's inner voice was screaming at this point. Rebecca was questioning who she was besides being a mother, wife, and housekeeper of her home.

When Rebecca looked at her life, she wanted something more. Her children were all old enough to take care of themselves. Rebecca took that opportunity to do some soul-searching and discovered her passion for running. She also discovered her need to make a change and find herself. Like so many of us, Rebecca

◇

was ready to find her identity and really discover her wants and desires.

It's not that there was anything wrong with her marriage, however, nothing was truly right. Rebecca looked at her life and decided that she wanted more—more happiness, more fulfillment, and more fun—and that was not going to happen if she stayed in that stale relationship. Rebecca filed for divorce, and over time, both her and her ex developed a good relationship, especially when it came to parenting their adult children.

As difficult as the decision had been for Rebecca, her true friends stood behind her and cheered her on. She was about to embark on a new journey that would make her feel more powerful and satisfied.

Although Rebecca's story was that about her marriage, it brings up a very important point about relationships in general. If *any* relationship, not just a romantic one, is not healthy for your mind, body, and soul, you need to get out of that situation. You have the power to decide if you want to be involved in that relationship or not. So many times women will comment their concern for their children, which is understandable. However, I believe that you can give your children no greater example than to show them your strength and sense of self if your existing relationship is unhealthy, to get out of that relationship.

***

One comment my friend made, which was a funny and valid point if you thought about it, was that marriages should be renewed between the fifteen- and twenty-year anniversaries. I remember when I got married. I knew people who were divorcing at twenty, twenty-five, and thirty plus years of marriage. At the time, I wondered how that could be. How could you be with someone for that much time and then walk away?

Now I honestly understand that. Marriage is work and quite often can easily become a partnership rather than a romantic marriage. Life takes over, and children, jobs, sports, pets, and many other distractions, which are all good, get in the way. It can be very challenging to keep your relationship alive when you are doing everything else.

I also think it is important to recognize that although divorce is a difficult decision, especially when you have children, it is important for two reasons. First, as an individual, you have the right to do what makes you happy and fulfilled. Second, you cannot make this decision with any regrets. You can make this decision with a sense of empathy for all those who are involved, but you do need to do what is best for you. You deserve to live your life.

As far as children are concerned, hopefully, your soon-to-be ex-husband will agree that the children's needs must come first. You are teaching your children a life skill about relationships, self-preservation, and strength. You have to acknowledge that it is a loss, but

◇

over time, you can hold space for this loss until you are strong enough to carry it. It will then slowly transform into your new reality.

The other factor is that people change. Take me for instance. I have certainly changed from who I was at age twenty-six when I was married. I am much more outspoken and not afraid to say how I feel. Always remember you are an individual first and deserve to be happy.

***

Claiming You

A relationship should offer balance, even when one person needs more support or compassion than the other. Any relationship with a partner, family member, or friend must give you a supportive, healthy environment that embraces you. There are many times when relationships are not fifty-fifty, however, even when the scale is tipped, a healthy relationship offers a nonjudgmental, safe place where you can just be you.

There is a great saying that I would like to share because it is about claiming your most powerful you. In order to do that, you need to protect your energy and use that energy wisely. If something or someone feels like a heavy weight on your shoulder, you are expending too much energy in dealing with that something or someone. In other words, give yourself permission to protect your energy for those people and times where it feels good to use it. Take on this motto:

To protect my energy, it is okay to change my mind.

To protect my energy, it is okay to cancel a commitment.

To protect my energy, it is okay to not pick up that phone call.

To protect my energy, it is okay to let go.

To protect my energy, it is okay to take a day off and do absolutely nothing.

To protect my energy, it is okay to speak up and ask for what I want.

To protect myself, it is okay to not share myself.

To protect my energy, it is okay not to feel guilty.

To protect myself, it is okay to find my passions and dreams.

To protect myself, it is okay to be alone and satisfied. (Lisa Marino)

CHAPTER 8

A Story about Trusting Your Intuition

What is intuition? You know, it's when you have that feeling in your gut. You can't really define why you may have that feeling, but it is an instinct. Instinct is an innate inclination toward a particular behavior or unconscious reasoning that propels us to act upon something without telling us how or why.

Before I begin this story, I need to preface it by saying, if there is one lesson to learn, that would be to trust your intuition. Sometimes we forget that, especially if we are feeling insecure or are with other people who may not have similar likes and dislikes as we do.

◇

Personally, I have always been an optimist or have tried to be. I have always tried to find the good in people and to give them the benefit of the doubt. However, not everyone is like that, and unfortunately, some have ulterior motives.

This is a story of following your heart and trusting your intuition. It is about a young woman who knows exactly what she wants, and although it may not be the *normal pattern* to some, it's her dream to follow.

Since a young age, Kyra has always enjoyed acting, and since the first time she stepped onto a stage, that was it. Her future was defined. She had many other passions, but life revolved around the theater. By high school, Kyra had been involved in approximately ten shows. She performed in school plays and community productions. She had virtually four straight years of acting, including summers, in shows or show-related work.

Let's fast-forward to graduation. Why was it so surprising that Kyra was going to follow her passion? Why did someone always have to ask, "What is your back up plan?" It frustrated and annoyed her.

Her biggest frustration was who was not supporting her. Surprisingly, her theater teacher and choral director, with whom she had spent and had given so much time to, were a some of her biggest critics. That did not stop Kyra. She knew two things. First, she had the talent. Second, she had the passion. She was going to follow her passion even if she had to do it alone.

One of her first challenges to overcome was the stereotype of attending college versus attending a true conservatory training program. Many people, even to this day, ask if she is taking any *real* classes. That's a bit insulting when you are working ten- to twelve-hour days.

There were challenges with this industry, but that's the case with all industries. However, if she had a passion for what she was doing, she would embrace the challenges because she loved it. The biggest challenge has been those people around her who are negative. Personally, she thinks they impose their fear of the unknown onto her.

Although that world, with its countless hours of practice and rehearsals, can be lonely, there is no place that Kyra would rather be. She values her alone time when she can think and center herself.

She is actively training and presently working toward her goal. There are some directors that love her and others that hate her before she opens her mouth. Kyra knows that she is just getting started. She is wise beyond her years. People can tell her how hard the business is. They ask her what will happen if she doesn't make it. Her response is to ask what would happen if she never tried. What if she didn't follow her passions? What if? What if? What if? That would be an unfortunate way to live.

Kyra followed her instinct and is happily pursuing her career as an actor. She listened to her intuition or gut and trusted her instincts. This is just one example. Has there ever been a time when your intuition yelled at you, loud and clear, to pursue or not to pursue something? Hopefully, you listened.

CHAPTER 9

Two Stories about Overcoming Challenges: Yin/Yang

There are two stories that I would like to share with you. Both stories deal with overcoming challenges, and were a direct result of being asked, "What does alone but not lonely mean to you?"

The first story takes on the challenge of dealing with loneliness. Before this friend could answer my question, he has to overcome and recognize the yang to the yin of the question. For this particular friend, the lonely part was a bit more challenging. Lonely to him was a

⬦

combination of isolation and solitude but could easily shift between both a positive and negative perspective.

Loneliness

The loneliest moments for me are usually when I'm around people. Other times include when my personal life may be challenging: I don't have immediate access to friends or family; traveling or out at business functions or restaurants. Often while traveling alone I am privy to others' discussions and hear great things that are happening or wonderful relationships others are having. It doesn't have to be necessarily positive either. They may be sharing a job loss, relationship woes, or the death of someone close to them. It's not the subject matter that raises the specter of loneliness; it's the interaction between people engaging emotionally with one another while I sit on the fringe, a sideline entity, unnoticed and for the most part ignored as social interaction swirls around me.

That sense of loneliness for me seems to ignite from a spark of hope that perhaps I'll be included, for the briefest of moments, and allows me to play with

◇

the idea that I have something of value to offer to the conversation. When that doesn't happen, I may ask myself, *Why should they bother with me? What, of value, do I have to offer to their conversation?*

These emotions are self-defeating, in that they cause many of us, including myself, to withdraw back into ourselves. We may internally fortify our resolve to not include ourselves, call it independence, and refuse to be vulnerable so that we don't risk getting hurt, but this compounds our sense of self-imposed isolation.

How do we respond? Well, in our minds we validate these feelings by focusing harder on our cell phones or the television in the corner and tell ourselves this is our choice. We take ourselves out of the equation, telling ourselves—convincing ourselves—that it doesn't matter.

We close our mind's eye to the idea that we have created this scenario and deny that angle of introspection because it would admit vulnerability, which society has deemed to be weakness. We soldier through it to repeat it or worse, to sink deeper into it and become more isolated.

***

As a side note, I would like to take a brief opportunity to talk about vulnerability as it was mentioned. So very often, vulnerability is deemed as a negative weakness on many levels. Because of my work as a life strategist, I urge the reader to look at vulnerability as a positive opportunity for growth. I agree that it can feel uncomfortable because it may represent a brand new thing. This is how you grow. When you carry yourself with confidence and purpose, yes, you may feel vulnerable, but you should also feel excited to try something new. Step outside of your comfort zone because that is how you continually grow and learn.

***

The Power of Being Alone

An old friend from college responded to the power of my book's title, *Alone but Not Lonely*, with a story about an incredible hike near the Grand Canyon about thirty-one years ago. What started as a day hike, to do something crazy and fun, turned into a soul-searching journey.

> *I started my day trip around 11 a.m., determined to get to the Ranch on the floor of the canyon, and went down the Bright Angel Trail off the South Rim. Made my way out the Plateau Point trail, and then continued on down to the Colorado River at the bottom of the Canyon. I calculated at that point I had gone about 15 miles. I remember the absolute euphoria I felt when I got to Phantom Ranch and dipped my bare feet in an icy creek. I then followed the trail along the river to the*

◇

footbridge, and when I saw the Kaibab, had to stop and mentally prepare. The Kaibab is approximately 5 miles long but also considered one of the steeper trails and rated for hikers as "expert".

Being young and stupid is a romantic notion in a book but I was miles from that sentiment, figuratively as well as physically. I had packed one small bag of jerky, a small bag of dried fruit, and two-quart bottles of water. I was Two miles up the Kaibab when the shadows started getting long when I took a break in the shade.

A Park Ranger walked by, stopped, and asked me if I was okay. Looking back, I remember the look on his face as though saying "Why are you here this late in the day with 3 plus miles to go?"

"Sure," I said, though wondering about that myself. With the sun starting to fade, I figured I better hustle. "Hustle" is a relative term and with a steep incline, 100 degree, and approaching the 20 mile mark after 8 hours, heat "hustle" wasn't really an option.

◇

I was still two miles from the top when I ran out of water and the sun was setting. The three months I spent out there taught me you couldn't fight the inevitable, so I sat down to watch a sunset I never got tired of seeing. I snapped a picture of a turkey vulture as it flew across the sunset. Needless to say, I chuckled at that as I accepted the fact that I wasn't going to make it to the top before dark. When I left that morning I recalled someone asking me if I had a flashlight, and youth and stupidity chimed in with, "No, but I'll be fine." Hindsight is a powerful teacher.

Night falls quickly in the canyon and a mile and a half from the top I was enveloped in complete and total darkness. I don't think I have experienced that kind of total absence of light. Dehydration, little food, 10 hours on the trails and outright exhaustion were driving some serious reflection on my situation. The trail was approximately 12 feet wide and that last mile and a half was taken in baby steps with my back edging along the cliff face, wondering what animal or wicked spirit might grab me at any moment and hurl me over the edge into oblivion.

◇

Due to some basic Boy Scout training, panic didn't set in entirely. However, night life in the canyon is active and the bats are numerous. And when you are in total darkness with a long fall just 10 feet away, you realize your position at the top of the food chain is tenuous at best.

The bats would pick up my bobbing head in their radar and do exploratory dives on my bobbing head, veering off with just enough space to feel the breeze of their wings. You didn't realize that they were there until the thump, thump, thump of their tiny little membranes were six inches from your head.

Again, the darkness was complete, absolute, cant see your hand in front of your face dark. With one exception. When I paused in my slow ascent, I looked up and saw the stars. Think of standing at the bottom of a deep can and looking up. The faint twinkle of a single star in that kind of situation was a beacon of motivation. As I gradually got closer to the top, and close enough to the top to make out the rim's silhouette against the night sky, I looked back and I was convinced there was someone coming up the trail behind

◇

me. The depletion of my bodily resources, the dark, and the bats had really messed with my head.

I took a break and looked back into the darkness of the canyon. I saw a singular light that at first I thought was a flashlight. Maybe the Park Ranger had turned around and wanted to make sure I wasn't passed out from heat exhaustion. But then the singular light became three, and started bouncing along the trail, when suddenly the split completely apart and went shooting into separate directions out into the canyon. Ninety percent of me is certain it was an hallucination. The other 10 percent has its doubts. The Canyon is steeped in Native American history and lore, with spirits, good and bad, inhabiting the canyon. I saw and heard some pretty funky stuff in the time I was there, and I came to believe that something as old as the canyon takes on a life of its own.

As I got to the top and came out onto the trail head all fear, paranoia, and exhaustion evaporated. It was after 11 p.m. I calculated that going down the Bright Angel, out the Plateau Point Trail, Phantom Ranch and up the South Kaibab,

◇

put me right at twenty-five miles, give or take, with the last mile and a half in total darkness.

Not bad. After the abysmal darkness below the rim, standing on the top with the moonlight filtering through the pine trees, I could see fairly well. It sounds sappy, but I raised my fists in victory and shouted into the canyon "Yes." To date it still ranks as one of my great achievements of sheer will.

I hitched a ride back to my dorm, took a long shower, and went to the bar. I shared my day with the bartender and he was incredulous at what I had accomplished. This is the first time I have ever totally related this story to someone. It is impossible to convey the intimidating beauty of that hike and the overall sense of Wow.

It was profoundly humbling yet empowering, and for me it certainly defines, with stark clarity, the power of alone but not lonely. Even with its' terrifying and exciting moments the sense of accomplishment stays with me almost 35 years later having pushed through the fear and exhaustion relying solely on my own internal resources.

◇

***

I want the reader to know that the same person shared both these very different stories of overcoming challenges. I want to share that with you because the stories are very different and contrasting. First, there was a true story of loneliness and the raw emotions associated with that. On the other hand, the second story told about the power of being alone, which brings up a very important message for all of us.

Life is not easy and there are days, times, and chapters of our journeys that are easier than others. These challenging times require us as human beings to rise up. Being able to look back and be totally honest with yourself is sometimes painful, but when you allow yourself time for reflection, you allow yourself time to be empathetic and to move on. It takes courage, my friends, to acknowledge it and to move forward.

***

CONCLUSION

In conclusion, "Alone but not lonely," is a powerful statement. I would like to highlight and recap several goals that I set out to share in this final chapter. It is truly my hope that by hearing these stories and applying the practical tools discussed, you will be able to begin your journey or continue your journey to find your passions, reclaim your identity, become unapologetically you, and, most of all, be comfortable and the most powerful when you are alone.

First, take some time to think about your identity. "Who would you be before the world told you who you should be?" It took me fifty-three years to really understand and be able to answer that question. Never lose sight of the things that excite you and maybe put a little fear in you as well.

Most importantly, whether you are in your twenties, thirties, forties, or fifties, always remember you are an individual and have your own needs as well. Take risks and allow yourself to dream big. As soon as I gave myself permission to be me, I began to let go of my own challenges.

Enjoy change. Change is growth and learning. Life is full of transitions and obstacles. You are the driver in your life. When you are truly happy, satisfied, and aligned, you will be there for others who lean on you, whether they are family, friends, or even people from your workplace. It comes down to aligning your mind, body, and spirit. Be gentle with yourself because you are in training to change past patterns.

Below is a summary of the tools I talked about. My challenge for you is that, as of today, you begin to make a shift. Every day, get into a routine that fits your schedule, even if it's only five to ten minutes.

1. Mind-Set

Mind-set is how we look at and react to things. In summary, mind-set is how we talk to ourselves. Quiet your mind from unnecessary, negative thoughts and replace them with positive, empowering beliefs. Then focus on the three-step process of dream it, believe it, and put it in action, to shift your beliefs and mind-set.

2. Lighten Your Load

This can be a hard habit to break if you are a person who always says, "Yes." Do you volunteer for everything? Are you the first one to jump in to help out? Choose wisely! Choose things that are important to you and give yourself permission to say *no*. Remember, this goes for people and relationships as well. If it feels heavy, let go of the weight.

3. The Five-Second Rule

Every time you start to have doubts or that little negative voice speaks, use the five-second rule. Count down, "Five, four, three, two, one," before reacting or responding to a situation.

4. Rituals

Morning

Start your day off right. Find your *alone* time to breathe, stretch, hydrate, and set your intentions for the day. Know exactly what you want for the day and go get it. Put yourself first, even if it lasts for only a few minutes. This is your time to gather your thoughts for you. I find it so interesting that as women, no matter what society says, we tend to put ourselves last. Even our pets come first! It has taken me fifty-three years to acknowledge my power to do just that.

Evening

Disconnect from the devices and think about three to five things from your day that made you happy.

5. Meditation

Whether you are a spiritual person or not, find a quiet place where you can close your eyes and focus on the quietness. Practice deep breathing for three to five minutes. If you enjoy meditation, there are some wonderful apps you can subscribe to.

6. Journaling

Bullet Journaling is a wonderful way to keep your calendar together with your thoughts. Save a few pages to write down your what you are grateful for, your daily affirmations, and/or words that make you feel powerful.

All in all, I want to leave you with this. You cannot go back and erase your stories, bad days, moments, memories, or experiences. However, you can move forward to process your stories and experiences so that you can grow from them and in return, carry them with ease. Healing begins when we stop running, deflecting, or hiding from the pain. Your alignment starts to happen when you acknowledge that you are ready to move forward and bring closure to whatever and whomever is there. It's not about forgetting the past, but it is about accepting that when you are alone, you are not lonely.

Very often, without even being aware of it, we compromise ourselves to please others. Whether this is family, friends, or bosses, it doesn't matter. You cannot compromise yourself to please others. Remind yourself who you are and what makes you happy. You do not need to compromise yourself to fit in. Those who truly support you will accept you for you. However, more importantly, you're not looking for that acceptance. The only validation that you need is from within. It's all about you standing as the most powerful you. I know that when you do claim your powerful self, you carry yourself stronger and more confidently.

My story really happened, and I have moved forward, recognizing the past as I look ahead toward an exciting future. My purpose in sharing this story is to let you know that you are not alone. I want to acknowledge others and to feel their stories. I want you to know that not only can you break the cycle but you also have the ability to reclaim and define your future. Create the life that you want to live and be unapologetically you at any age.

With that being said, let me leave you with my final thoughts:

Learn to be alone without being lonely.

Learn to appreciate your beauty without finding fault.

Learn to love yourself without the love of others. (H.r.d.)

Learn to know your self-worth without asking for the opinions of others. (R.j.m.)

ABOUT THE AUTHOR

Robin Meyers is a mother of three adult children. She resides in the Washington DC area with her husband. As a life strategist, Robin's goal is to empower women, all over the world, to find their passions and to follow their visions at any age. Through life there are many transitions, but what matters most is that women realize that their self-worth is non-negotiable.

Robin has her master of science in molecular genetics from Case Western Reserve University but was never passionate about that field. Instead, she became an educator, mentor, speaker, and founder of Navigate & Empower LLC.

At age fifty-three, Robin has never felt stronger, happier, or more satisfied and, in turn, wants to share her training and personal story to support all of you. To learn more about her, please visit her website at <u>www.</u><u>robinmeyers.life</u>.

Being alone is a powerful time to reflect, plan, and quiet the outside noises so you can let your creativity soar. Reclaim your identity and be unapologetically you!

COMING SOON

Beginning in 2018, I look forward to sharing the following sequels to this book:

Alone but Not Lonely for Entrepreneurs

Alone but Not Lonely for Teens

Alone but Not Lonely for Actors

Alone but Not Lonely for Divorce

Alone but Not Lonely for Mothers

Alone but Not Lonely for Silvers

If you are interested in sharing your story or would like Robin at your next event, please contact Robin at www.robinmeyers.life.

NOTES

The following pages are left to take notes and answer questions from the book. Make lists, start a journal or even answer: Who is ..... (replace with your name)?

I hope you enjoy this journey and always feel free to email me at **robin@navigate-empower.com** with any questions.

NOTES

NOTES

NOTES

Printed in the United States
By Bookmasters